Leadership Moments

with Larry

BY DR. LARRY LITTLE

"Leadership is found in the moments of life."

A Note From Larry

Leadership can be found in the most unusual places and in the most unassuming people. It's not about leading a large organization or directing a monumental project. Leadership is found in the moments of life. It can be discovered in people that we would never consider "leaders" in the traditional sense.

I have the privilege of walking with executives who lead at the highest levels of corporations and organizations. I have journeyed with entrepreneurs and leaders of companies of all sizes. I am thankful for those opportunities to listen and learn from some of the best leaders on the planet. Likewise, there are those moments when I learn from someone who would never be considered a "great leader" in the strictest definition of the word. It is in those moments with those people that I have gained life nuggets that I will carry with me forever.

The following pages are filled with Leadership Moments from people of all walks of life. I have shared these moments through the past several years with thousands of people worldwide through my weekly email.

I hope that that this compilation will serve as an encouragement to you as you seek to lead others, but most importantly I hope it is a reminder that you can make a difference in the lives of others.

Larry

Cheers to New Beginnings!

Well... here we go. A new year brings another opportunity to set goals, build strategic plans and develop action items. Recently, I had the opportunity to be challenged by two leaders in one day. Their words put things into perspective. The first was a wise young leader who made a statement that took me by surprise. He said, " You can have the best intentions but without correct direction you will accomplish nothing." Then another leader made this statement, " If you want to be extraordinary, you have to live your life on purpose".

Through the years I have seen men and women who had great intentions but no direction. What would happen if we decided to create clarity of direction for our lives both professionally and personally? What if our intentions were based on why we exist instead of what we intend to gain? What if we lived our lives with purpose to accomplish that "why" instead of allowing life to "just happen"?

The truly successful leaders will be those who spend their year increasing their influence and investment in others. I want to have more than just good intentions this year. I want to march purposefully in the direction of becoming a successful leader.

Choose to know the where and why of your leadership and life this year and you will make a difference!

Live It Out

"I was talking with a seasoned leader who is also a friend.

We were talking about career paths, strategic planning and the on-going pursuit of the "next thing". He looked at me and said, "You know, at some point you have to know when to just 'live it out'." He continued, "If we are always in pursuit of the next thing, we will miss the beauty found in our current set of circumstances."

It made me stop and ask a question. Am I so busy chasing the vision that I am missing all the incredible things happening all around me? If I slowed down long enough, I would see relationships that I cherish and need. I would soak in the calmness of a quiet night or the ability to eat a delicious piece of chocolate pie. I would treasure authentic conversation. I would learn more about our team and enjoy the journey of working together. I would appreciate the beauty of the lake or the therapy of the beach.

I am not diminishing the reality that many leaders are experiencing personal or professional stress. Many are in a chaotic or crisis season of life. However, my friend reminded me of the value of slowing down and taking in the things that matter in our lives.

The ability to notice the beauty in the midst of busyness is a discipline that will allow us to lead with vision and insight. I think I'll take a moment to appreciate the atmosphere around me. Right now, I'm really enjoying a wonderful cup of coffee.

Choose to be intentional about "just living life out" and you will make a difference.

Love Yourself First

"How can I lead someone else if I am not leading myself well?"

"You have to love yourself before you can truly love someone else." A strange concept for many, but this was the advice of an aged and seasoned leader... my dad. With little formal education he has earned his degree through the rigors of life. As an entrepreneur, he struggled through the ups and downs of owning a small business, making his fortune in something other than financial gains. My Dad has become rich in relationships. He gives more than he probably should and thus he has garnered the respect and friendship of many. Now, looking back over his life, he tells me "you must love yourself first". Really? That seems inconsistent with who he is... until you take a deeper look at this principle of leadership.

How can I truly love someone when I don't love myself? Likewise, how can I lead someone else, if I'm not leading myself well? The concept seems to contradict the theory of leading through humility. However, quite the opposite is true. If I am confident in my strengths and weaknesses, then I am better equipped to lead others in their strengths and through their weaknesses. The path to being secure in our leadership begins with the reality that we must lead ourselves well. That means developing an understanding of who we are and more importantly why we are leading.

In leading myself well, I discover my purpose and remain authentic to my core values. This makes me a stronger leader with the ability to influence others on a much broader scale. And at the end of our journey of leadership the most significant contribution we leave is not our financial portfolio but the lives that we have influenced in a positive way.... and it begins with loving and leading ourselves well... just ask my dad.

Choose to lead yourself well and you will make a difference!

Keep Dancing

I was meeting with a close friend who leads hundreds of people in multiple locations. As we were talking he said, "Have you ever noticed when small children are in the presence of music they generally love to dance? And when senior adults are around music they generally love to dance?"

He continued, "Something happens to us between being a small child and a senior adult —we lose our ability and desire to dance." The burdens of life, the responsibility of leading, the heaviness of a gray, imperfect world can steal our ability to dance.

Can you hear the music? Listen to the beauty around you. You have been given an incredible opportunity to lead others. Hear the sounds of those you love and of those who love you. Embrace the beat of potential that greets you every morning. Pay attention to the rhythm of growth that surrounds you. Take note of the harmony of diversity that creates progress.

Go ahead...tap your foot. Here comes the sway. You can do it! Allow yourself to move and to feel the joy.

Get on the dance floor of life! Let yourself experience the wonder of life, of loving, and of leading.

Choose to dance and you will make a difference!

"Hear the sounds of those you love and of those who love you. Embrace the beat of potential that greets you every morning. Pay attention to the rhythm of growth that surrounds you. Take note of the harmony of diversity that creates progress."

It's Worth It

There are those times that I ask myself; is it really worth it? Why should I invest in others? This world is full of poor leaders who are selfish, so does my small influence actually matter?

I find answers in the most unlikely places. Meet Nolan. He is the manager at a chain shoe store. He met us at the door with a warm smile and a "welcome". He served us as we looked for shoes. He wasn't just interested in selling shoes; he authentically wanted to learn about us. He was knowledgeable about his craft, but he demonstrated much more than shoe IQ. He listened to us, learned a bit about who we were and then asked questions that were sincere and relevant.

It was a refreshing reminder that no matter how small our circle of influence may be, we as leaders have a responsibility to continue the journey of influencing others in a positive direction. We lead because it is who we are, not what we do. We care because we are called to serve others. We influence through our authentic desire to speak into the lives of others.

Nolan is a young leader who is doing just that. Yes, it is important to continue the struggle, keep fighting to build strong solid leaders and investing in those around us.

Why should I invest in others? Nolan reminded me that it is because of the opportunity that I have every day to make a difference!

Judgment Road

"Life lessons don't have to become life sentences."

I was skeptical. Thinking about the past and predicting the future, I was walking down the road of judgment and writing this person off. That's when an executive stopped me in my tracks. She said, "You know, Life Lessons don't have to become Life Sentences".

It was like hitting me in the gut. As I remembered lessons that I have learned the hard way in my life, I realized the truth of her statement. We all fall and at times fail.

Maybe it's a poor decision made in a vulnerable or weak moment. Maybe it's a reaction based on our fear or greed. Maybe it's lashing out in anger. Maybe it is simply not slowing down to make a wise decision.

The truth is, we all have experienced failure in our lives. The most important decision is found in what we choose to learn from our mistakes. Some will allow their mistakes to define them.

Others will continue to live in their mistakes and repeat them over and over.

But we can choose to respond differently.

We can choose to learn from our mistakes. We can choose to allow our missteps to make us stronger and to make us wiser as leaders. In fact, history proves that great leaders were those who learned from their mistakes.

Sometimes we are quick to pass judgment on those who fall or make mistakes. My friend's wisdom causes me to pause and remember that learning a life lesson can be the conduit for growth and strength for a leader.

The next time I start down the judgment road, I will strive to remember her words of wisdom.

When we choose to be slow to judge we can make a difference!

Sister Rosemary

I recently had the opportunity to meet with leaders from across the world. I listened and learned from some of the best of the best in the leadership arena. There was one who struck a chord with my soul.

Her name is Sister Rosemary Nyirumbe and she was one was of TIME's 100 Most Influential People in 2014. That is not why I was so touched by her. Sister Rosemary is a Catholic nun who has dedicated her life to helping girls formerly held captive by warlords and the rebel army in Uganda. These girls were abducted, raped, tortured and forced to kill their own family members.

In addition to providing a safe harbor for the girls, Sister Rosemary has given them the ability to support themselves. She offers job training in tailoring, catering and other skills. She said that she teaches the girls to sew and begins the lessons by telling them that the needles they are holding do something very special. They take pieces of broken and torn fabric and sew them together to make something beautiful. She tells them that they can sew their torn lives into something beautiful and meaningful.

While her story is incredibly inspiring, her last words are the ones that I will remember. She said, "Thank you for bringing me here, but next time, bring two of my girls and allow them to tell their own story". She was concerned with allowing her girls to grow as leaders and influencers. That is the characteristic of a great leader.

Sister Rosemary is doing more than just offering a helping hand.

She is developing girls who are becoming leaders with the passion and ability to truly make a difference.

15

"Don't mistake brilliance for direction and purpose."

Experts *vs.* Leaders

"**H**e is brilliant." "She is incredibly intelligent." Those are words we would all like to hear about ourselves. Let's face it; we all want to be smart. Its normal to desire to be seen as an expert in your given field of study or work. Sometimes I think we put too much emphasis on IQ competency and not enough on EQ capacity. A senior executive was talking with me about developing leaders within his organization when he said: *"Don't mistake brilliance for direction and purpose".*

So many times we look for experts when what we really need are leaders. Leaders know how to gather experts and access knowledge. Experts know how to dispense knowledge about a certain subject. Both are important but only one can accomplish things greater than his or her abilities. I have witnessed countless "smart" experts who are not effective leaders outside of their own technical expertise. Many times, when we find all of our value in our technical competency, we set ourselves up for a narcissistic leadership style that centers on ourselves.

The strongest and most effective leaders are those who surround themselves with others who are smarter in some area. These leaders realize the importance of driving direction and purpose in an organization, team or a home.

Choose to not always have to be the smartest person in the room and you will make a difference.

The Beach

I love the beach. It is a place of renewal for me and many of the major decisions of my life have been determined while spending time at the coast. While we have our favorite beach getaway location, we never visit the same beach twice. The travel path, our condominium, the parking lot in which we leave our car, the familiar restaurants, all may be the same each time we journey to the beach, but the beach itself is never the same.

Every wave at the beach is unique and one of a kind. The shore line is in constant transformation with each tide. Sandbars come and go as do the beautiful creatures who call the ocean their home.

Will there be seaweed in the surf today? How strong is the ever-flowing undertow? Will the winds produce wading ponds with small ripples or incredibly fierce and dangerous surf where no man can safely swim?

Likewise, leading is an ever-changing and ever-challenging opportunity. Some days the surf is smooth and relaxing while other days bring the turmoil of a raging sea.

Understanding this truth allows us to be intentional. We should enjoy the calm waters, but we must realize that our environment is ever changing. We can persevere through the storms because we know that our situation will change.

Celebrate the constant change of your life and leadership.

Choose to remember that you never visit the same day twice and you will make a difference!

Creating A Culture

The problem with creating a culture is that you cannot do it. The word "creating" literally means "To cause something to come into being." Unless you are standing up a new venture, the culture within your organization, company, or team is already in motion. This being the case, the question then becomes, "What kind of culture are you leading?"

Upon examination of your team's culture, you may choose to change the direction in which it is headed. The first step in this process is to take a long hard look at yourself. Are you modeling the culture that you want to instill in others? Are you willing to invest the time, energy, and effort to model and teach the new direction you have chosen? Are you willing to consistently hold your team accountable for implementing this new direction?

One word of caution, do not attempt to change the culture unless you are totally committed to the endeavor. A lack of follow-through or intentionality may cause more harm than good.

Make sure your choice is the result of a well thought-out plan to change the course of your culture and you will make a difference!

Not My Stuff

> *"Choosing to focus on **my** stuff has allowed me to become more focused and effective as a leader."*

She is a brilliant, highly successful executive working for a large educational system. Her track record reveals a path of success in virtually every area that she has led.

In the Make a Difference system vernacular, she is a strong Lion. She is sought after and respected for her vision, leadership and educational acumen. I asked her, in light of all of her success, to name something that she has learned about herself.

She said, "One of the most powerful things I am learning is NMS." I asked her to explain.

"It stands for Not My Stuff. I have the tendency to try to fix things that I don't need to fix. The result is that I over commit myself and thus increase my stress and decrease my productivity. Choosing to focus on **my** stuff, has allowed me to become more focused and effective as a leader."

As leaders, we are wired to recognize areas that could be improved. We recoil when we see mediocrity or underperformance. Our instincts may be to jump in and fix the issue, to make it excellent.

However, doing so can lead to frustration, boundary issues and, ultimately, burn out. While there is no doubt that apathy and poor performance are at epidemic levels in our work culture today, we must realize that taking on too many issues will undermine our ability to lead with excellence.

It takes discipline and determination to identify our big rocks, to attack and to stay focused on those goals and objectives. The wise leader's challenge is one worth taking.

Choose to realize what is NMS and you will make a difference!

The Mirror

He is recognized as one of the leading experts in his field and works for one of the largest companies in the world in their industry.

This Brazilian leader has a global presence and was offered the opportunity to lead a premier leadership team with members sitting literally in multiple countries across the planet.

The team gathered in Spain for their initial meeting with this leader. This could have been a time when he displayed his knowledge and expertise to his new team. He could have pontificated on how things were going to change under his leadership.

He did none of these things. Instead he was authentic and vulnerable. He realized the incredible responsibility he had, to lead the team. He knew that it was up to him to represent and support each member of his new team.

Instead of making this moment about him he chose to make it about them.

This is what he told them: "**When I look in the mirror I will see each of you. I am merely a reflection of you. You are my mirror**".

He explained to me that it was important for him to take the focus off of himself and communicate to the team that he was "there for each of them".

He said that he took the role because he truly believed he could help each leader on this team to be successful.

This leader is creating a culture of humility and teamwork and servant leadership.

His determination to put his team first will result in greater productivity, increased efficiency and desired outcomes.

When I look into the mirror I will see each of you. I am merely a reflection of you. You are my mirror.

It took courage and integrity for this leader to display such authenticity in his very first leadership team meeting.

It is a rare approach but a highly effective one.

Choose to represent and reflect those you lead and you will make a difference.

Focus on the Future

A wise leader taught me, "Experience alone is not always the best teacher."

This is especially true when making decisions about the future.

If we base our decisions solely on past experiences, we limit ourselves from the possibilities of new and creative ideas.

"We have always done it that way," or "It's never been done that way before," are phrases that

will stifle growth and ingenuity in any organization.

What if the Wright Brothers had allowed their past experiences with flying to dictate their future decisions? While they used the past as part of the process, their creativity and ingenuity pushed them upward.

If Thomas Edison had allowed his past failures to stump him, we would all be in the dark.

Don't allow the past to have the majority vote in your decision making process.

Stay open to new ideas, uncomfortable options, and unknown risks. The results may surprise you.

Stay focused on the future with an eye for ingenuity and you will make a difference!

Red Stars

Let me introduce you to Ellie. She is driven, competitive and determined. Ellie is on a quest. Ellie is five years old and is working hard to obtain the Red Star. With the Red Star comes additional privileges and rewards. The Red Star is achieved through accomplishing specific goals at home. She charts her accomplishments and works hard to reach her goals. She celebrates her victories and determines to keep on trying when she doesn't reach her goals.

Goals are what move us. They can create accountability and give honest feedback to our progress. They give us purpose and meaning and keep us from living in stagnated apathy. We all need something to pursue, to reach for, and to accomplish. The ultimate goal should be for us to get better every day of our lives. This means identifying those things in our lives that we are not pleased with and setting a goal to improve them. When we accomplish a step toward reaching our goals, we should celebrate the small victory. When we stumble and fail to reach our goal, we should be determined to keep on trying.

Ellie is racking up the Red Stars and learning a valuable lesson about how goals can benefit her. Begin identifying goals on a consistent basis in your life. Chase them and allow them to hold you accountable.

Choose to set goals for life and you will make a difference!

Bear Claws

They looked and smelled so good.

I was picking up an order of donut holes when I noticed a batch of bear claw pastries cooking.

If you are an advocate for eating correctly, I apologize for my unhealthy fall from the wagon of good health.

I couldn't help but comment to the worker, "Those bear claws look so good!" She responded, "Wait just a minute".

Then she went over to those brown greasy sizzling pastries and pulled a big delicious warm bear claw out of the fryer.

She wrapped it up and with a smile on her face said "Here you go... It's on the house. See you again soon!"

In today's culture of self-preservation and the "what's in it for me" mindset, the donut lady's unsolicited gift was refreshing.

It was also a reminder that leadership sometimes requires us to give a little extra.

Because of her little extra gift of a wonderful bear claw, the donut lady insured that I would visit her shop again soon.

Choose to give beyond what is expected and you will make a difference!

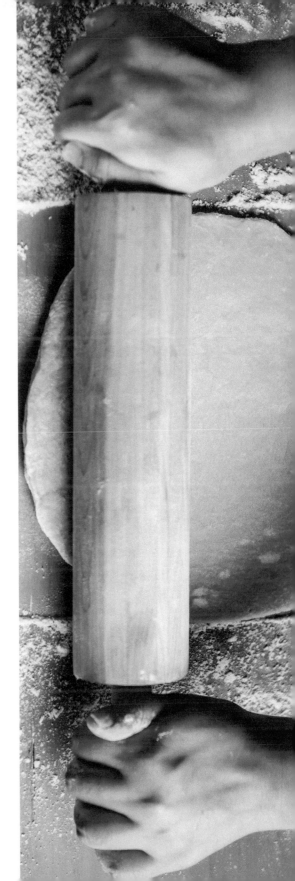

"Leadership sometimes requires us to give a little extra."

Face to Face

"You're doing what?" I asked with disbelief. I was talking to an executive and couldn't believe what I was hearing. He had just gotten back from a grueling trip across several continents.

The trip itself takes 30 hours, not to mention the travel and stress upon arriving. He repeated, "I'm going back overseas next week." He continued, "Some things cannot be accomplished with technology. I need to visit each plant and I need to look my team members in the eye. It is crucial that I build trust with this team."

This wise executive reminded me that effective communication is not just about spewing information to someone. It is about investment, respect and trust. Those team members will have a new level of appreciation and respect for this executive who demonstrated sacrifice in order to come to them.

Ask yourself the question, "With whom do I need to have a face-to-face conversation?"

Choose to make the time, energy and effort to have an in-person, one-on-one conversation with those who are important in your life and you will make a difference.

The Masterpiece

"The creators of these works of art were intentional about leaving their message for others."

On a scale of one-to-ten, my knowledge and expertise in historical art, architecture, and statues hovers around negative six. Recently, as we toured Italy, I had the opportunity to learn just how much I didn't know about this important part of world history. While we were immersed in the culture and art of this wonderful country full of historical treasures, one thing began to stand out to me.

All of the art, sculptures, and buildings had one common dominator. Each creation was designed with intentionality. In other words, each piece held a purpose that has been preserved for centuries. Some of the work held a political message, some a spiritual message, and some held more narcissistic, self-serving messages. But the creators of these works of art were intentional about leaving their message for others.

As we ponder our leadership, we have to ask, "What message am I leaving?" We are responsible for how we lead our teams and our family and friends. Each day we add another paint stroke, chisel another portion of our sculpture, or add a design detail of architectural importance.

This message is unique and we are responsible for its content. We must remember that we are creating a lasting message through our leadership masterpiece.

Remember, the question is not "if" but "what kind of" message you and I are sending as a leader. Those who choose to live without purpose in their lives and in their leadership efforts will surely send a message of apathy or of self-centered narcissism.

Yet, those who choose to live and lead with purpose will create a legacy of leadership that will last well beyond their time on this earth.

Choose to create a leadership masterpiece that is intentional and you will make a difference!

True Leadership

While attending a leadership forum in Washington D.C. recently, I had the opportunity to sit with leaders from large and small countries from around the world.

I listened as they shared their concerns about the issues affecting their homelands. I was moved by the passion and the sincere concern these individuals had for the people of their country.

The schedule was fast-paced, and required back-to-back meetings over three days.

Leading the meetings was a leader with years of experience in global concerns, and who serves our country on a daily basis. There was great diversity in the languages spoken, the issues presented, the style of clothes worn, and the distance traveled. However, I observed two things that were not diverse within the meetings.

The first was the forum leader—he gave intense attention to each delegation. He listened, asked questions, showed genuine concern, and stayed engaged during every meeting.

While he did not have the ability to solve all of their issues, he left no doubt that each foreign leader had been heard.

The second observation was that after being heard, each country's leader demonstrated appreciation. The mutual respect in the room was quite powerful.

What would happen if we as leaders took the time to demonstrate genuine concern for those we lead? What if we authentically listened to and engaged those with whom we have different opinions and beliefs?

Think of the results of offering sincere appreciation to those who follow us, as well as to those who lead us.

True leadership occurs when others feel heard and appreciated.

Choose to be a true leader and you will make a difference!

> *"He listened, asked questions, showed genuine concern, and stayed engaged during every meeting."*

Legacy

It was a life changing decision. She was literally at a cross roads in her career. This seasoned executive has years of experience and is being sought after by another top-notch organization.

As we were discussing her options she said, "I think it's important to make my decision on something other than money. While the packages are comparable, I want to use this as an opportunity to pursue my legacy."

When I asked her what she meant, she responded, "I have a passion for helping others to obtain what they see as impossible. As I head into the second season of my career,

I want to intentionally work toward my legacy".

What will others say about you at the end of your days on this earth? Each one of us is living a legacy. We are defining how others will define our lives by how we are living in the present.

The decisions we are making on a daily basis will cumulatively add up to the legacy that we will leave.

Choosing to be intentional about our decisions will allow us to make a difference in the lives of those we love, live with and lead.

Coffee Maker

I consider myself a good listener, but I was sure that I had missed something. "Could you repeat that again?" I asked.

The reply was the same... "Who is going to make our coffee?" I was meeting with a leader who had recently made a hard call to release a mid level manager within the organization. Upon meeting with this manager's team, the leader was prepared to hear various concerns or issues around the departure of this long-term manager. Instead the most pressing question he received was, "Who is going to make our coffee?"

While this response gave affirmation to this leader that he made the right call, it serves as an important reminder to us as leaders. What do our leaders really bring to their teams? Are they simply filling a role with apathy toward your organization? Are they so comfortable that productivity and leadership is lacking? What 'value add' is received from their managing others? Are they in the right seat on the team?

Now take a moment to ask yourself the hard questions... what value are you bringing to your team? Are you authentically investing in the growth and development of other leaders? Are you so comfortable that you have forgotten how to take risks and challenge the status quo? Are you leading with inspiration and vision?

Take a moment to examine your personal and professional relationships. Are they intentional and purposeful? One of the greatest dangers we face as leaders is the temptation to become stagnant. Are you leading effectively in all areas of your life... or are you just making coffee?

Choose to stay fresh in your leadership and you will make a difference!

Guard Your Words

It was an important meeting with the leadership team. The issue was crucial and complicated.

For the first half of the meeting, there was silence....from the leader. He did not say a word, but instead, listened. Then he asked a series of questions and follow up questions.

One of the myths that plague leaders today is the idea that leadership means talking. Leading a meeting does not mean dominating or controlling the meeting. Leaders who are slow to speak are those who make the strongest decisions.

A wise executive once told me, "I guard my words very carefully and try to speak with intention and purpose."

Allowing others to speak up is a sign of a self-confident and mature leader. Having to always give commands and direction is a sign of a weak leader or a weak team. When there is room for discussion and debate, relationships grow both personally and professionally.

Choose to allow others to speak up and you will make a difference!

The Presentation

The table was set. The lighting was adjusted. The music was playing. You might think that I am describing a dinner party, but I am actually describing a recent business presentation.

The two presenters knew that this was an important opportunity and they set the tone of excellence from the moment we walked into the room. Details were considered and it was obvious that the presentation we were experiencing had been well thought through and developed. My appreciation for their effort immediately caused me to pay closer attention to their pitch.

The above experience is becoming rare in today's culture. In our race to meet our calendar deadlines, or accomplish the next task I wonder if we sometimes sacrifice the art of excellence for the convenience of immediacy. If I am not careful, I find myself running at a pace that jeopardizes the quality of my leadership. Consequently, details are lost, the extras that set us apart are forgotten, people are put on the back burner and ultimately my effectiveness is diminished.

This presentation reminded me of the importance of taking time to prepare well and to offer a high quality experience. As leaders, it is our responsibility to demonstrate a high caliber of execution in all that we do.

Choose to take the time to lead with a tone of excellence and you will make a difference.

Fake News

> ## "As leaders, there is no substitute for basic, clear communication with those we lead."

It's my profession. I am a communicator. You would think that I would know better. But, I did it again.

In an attempt to create a bit of excitement and anticipation, I instead created chaos.

Here is what happened: We may have an opportunity to allow one of our sites to experience an upgrade in facilities.

This seems like a very benign event that everyone should look forward to experiencing.

That is, until I sent a cryptic email telling our team to be on the look out for some exciting news coming their way.

Thus started the guessing, gossip and rumor train. Before I knew it, our team had become the poster child for "fake news".

Moreover, it was all because of my poor effort at generating a bit of fun. Once I realized my mistake, I communicated the facts as clearly and simply as possible.

As leaders there is no substitute for basic clear communication with those we lead. Our team thrives when we are transparent with our data, knowledge and plans.

What may seem like over communication to us feels like clarity to those we lead.

When there is uncertainty, lack of clarity or cryptic information, the result will always be chaos and confusion.

I have learned my lesson (at least for the moment).

Choose to over communicate with clarity and you will make a difference.

"The road of life is paved with flat squirrels who couldn't make a decision."

Squirrels

"The road of life is paved with flat squirrels who couldn't make a decision."

When my friend, Moriah shared the above quote with me, it instantly became one of my favorites.

Decision-making is a topic that comes up over and over as our team at Eagle continues to walk with leaders.

I was recently talking with an executive who was struggling with a member of his team who simply could not or would not make a decision. He consequently removed this leader from his team.

This seasoned leader shared with me, "If I refuse to make this hard call, I penalize our team and ultimately our entire organization."

I realize that there is a time for collaboration and listening in the decision making process. Expending the time and energy to understand how we, along with those we lead, make decisions is crucial to the success of any leader.

However, once the data has been collected and the collaboration has been completed, we must have the courage to make the call.

Rest assured, there will always be those on the sidelines who are quick to criticize your decisions, especially if things don't turn out to suit them.

The truth is that we all will make bad decisions from time to time. If we find ourselves making more poor calls than successful ones, then it may take time to assess how and why we are making those decisions.

"We must have the courage to make the call."

Refusing to make a decision because of our fear of failure or from a lack of awareness of the urgency of the situation are signs of a selfish leader.

This lack of leadership causes frustration and confusion from those we lead.

Leaders who are willing to own the risk of making the wrong call are those who garner respect and appreciation from those within their circle of influence.

Choose to courageously make a decision.... don't be a flattened squirrel.... and you will make a difference!

Connected

our companies we have sophisticated programs to track, calculate, monitor, and spew tons of data at us 24 hours a day. We have the ability to communicate instantly across the globe. We can see, hear and talk to anyone at any time.

It's ridiculous. I'm watching my computer screen on the TV. I can do the same with my iPhone, iPad, and who knows what else. We hold these devices in our hand and get instant results on literally any topic we can imagine. In

I recently read an interview with Steve Jobs. He said "We're already in information overload. No matter how much information the Web can dish out, most people get far more information than they can assimilate anyway." That was in 1996. Can you imagine the amount of information we

are getting today?

With this over load of technology and information, we struggle more than ever with simple interactions like talking and connecting and listening. We run at this incredible pace.

We achieve tasks that we could only dream of a few years ago...and yet our teams are frustrated and our personal relationships are struggling.

In the same interview Steve said this "We're born, we live for a brief instant, and we die. It's been happening for a long time. Technology is not changing it much - if at all." We have so much information that it is ridiculous.

The truth is that the only thing that can authentically impact lives is choosing, in this "brief instant" called life, to reach out and make a difference.

The Catfish and the Cod

A CEO and friend recently taught me the lesson of the Cod and the Catfish.

He said that fisherman discovered that when cod are captured and put in a live well they become lethargic and die before the fishing boats return to shore. This makes the cod useless and inedible.

The fisherman then put catfish in the live well with the cod and they discovered something remarkable. The catfish poke, prod, nip and totally aggravate the cod so that upon return the cod are alive and well.

The truth is that we need people in our lives that think differently than we do. I find myself becoming frustrated with those who are difficult for me to engage. They may poke with criticism, prod with unending questions, nip with sarcasm or totally aggravate with their personality style. However, if I take a step back, I realize that learning to navigate difficult people makes me a stronger leader.

Take a minute and think about the catfish in your life. Instead of allowing the frustration of their behavior to dominate your thoughts, think about how you can grow from your relationship with them. Leadership is not for those who tend to give up and quit.

Choose to learn from your catfish and you will make a difference!

Celebrate

Our country was formed from, among other things, a need for self-expression, freedom of speech, and religion as well as the pursuit of liberty. We have seen success and we have experienced setbacks. We have led the world in certain areas and yet still have much to learn. We are a nation of overachievers and at times underachievers. Some call us a melting pot of the world.

It's important that we take time to celebrate the freedom of our country: that we honor those in our military who choose and have chosen to sacrifice so that we might experience life, liberty and the pursuit of our dreams, that we celebrate our forefathers who had the courage and insight to create the Declaration of Independence. I am grateful and choose to celebrate the fact that we were founded as "one nation under God."

What does all of this celebration have to do with leadership? Everything! We are a country of leaders. Through the years, men and women have stepped out of their comfort zone and led with courage, honor and integrity. We are a country that is still learning and we are a country that is still leading. Our leaders are found both in the private and public sectors. They are found in the large corporations, government agencies, educational institutions, and small family owned businesses. They are diverse and they are determined. They love their country, their families and their God.

We celebrate our country's leaders- those from our past who have given us our freedom, those in the present who allow us to continue to pursue our dreams, and those in the future who will keep our country free. We celebrate and we say, *"Thank you leaders– for making a difference!"*

The Glacier

A strong wind was blowing and rain mixed with sleet was falling. As we approached Juneau, Alaska our trip to Herbert Glacier was in question.

My wife was convinced that there was no way that we were going to board a helicopter and travel to the top of a mountain glacier in these conditions.

I, being a bit of a risk taker, continued to pursue the possibility of taking our adventure flight to Herbert.

After conferring with the professionals who were to lead the trip, we were assured it was safe to take the flight.

After a long conversation, we decided to take the risk and embark on an excursion to the giant glacier.

A strong leader who served our country and led thousands of military men and women said the biggest obstacle to learning and growing is fear.

He stated that we allow fear to polarize us and keep us from fulfilling our dreams and leading well.

We are afraid of failing, losing our job, making mistakes, not measuring up and the list goes on and on.

When we live in a culture of fear we cheat others and ourselves from achieving and growing as individuals and leaders.

I realize that there is a difference in taking a calculated risk and being unwise in our actions. However, many times, we allow fear to drive our decisions and thus our behavior.

> *"When we live in a culture of fear, we cheat others and ourselves from growing as leaders."*

Leadership is at times scary. All of us experience fear. The secret to strong leadership is to acknowledge our fear and then develop a plan to navigate it.

I'm so glad that we overcame our fear and experienced the thrill of walking on the Herbert Glacier. It is an experience I will remember for the rest of my life.

Choose to be fearless in your leadership and you will make a difference.

Summer

It is summer and it's hot. In the south this means temperatures reaching high double digits with humidity to match. It is during this season that things tend to slow down a bit as people vacation and try to stay cool. While rest is important and slowing down is necessary for endurance, there is more value to this process than meets the eye. I have observed that leaders who are successful, are those who know how to navigate the slow times as well as the fast times.

I was talking with an executive who has the unique ability to identify and place leaders effectively in his organization. As we talked, I made an observation that one of his direct reports, who has a substantial leadership role, rarely slows down long enough to invest in his own leadership development. He operates in high gear year round. While he accomplishes many tasks, he is not leading with intentionality. There are no leaders being developed under his guidance and he is not investing in his own growth as a leader.

The wise and seasoned executive with whom I was talking said of the above-mentioned leader, "That is why he will never progress to a CEO." While he is great at tasks, he is not growing as a leader and this will hinder his ability to be successful at the next level.

Take a moment and analyze your growth as a leader. Look for opportunities to invest in your leadership in the slow times as well as the fast times.

This week, take the opportunity to slow down and invest in growing as a leader and you will make a difference!

The Parking Lot

"Leadership is about choosing to take a risk even when you might be misunderstood or misjudged."

I was in the parking lot of a local thrift store unloading my car with items we were donating. Oblivious to my surroundings, I was hunched over in my car trying to reach the last items. That's when it happened.

I heard someone running toward me and yelling. A million thoughts ran through my mind..."what is happening?" "Is someone being attacked?" "Am I about to be assaulted?" "Should I fight or flight?" "Do I get involved?"

As I climbed out of the car I saw this young lady running and reaching out toward me! The adrenaline rushed as I tried to assess the crisis occurring in front of my eyes.

Was someone chasing her? Was there a weapon involved? Should I defend myself or save the girl?

The young woman ran right by me and grabbed... my buggy. My lack of focus had prohibited me from noticing that my buggy had started rolling. It was only inches away from crashing into my car when she stepped in front of it.

She said, "I saw that it was about to hit your car". Relieved that I did not have a large dent in my car from the runaway buggy, I thanked her and she continued on her way.

Leadership is about reaching out unconditionally to those around you. It is choosing to take a risk even when you might be misunderstood or misjudged. It is taking action for the benefit of others.

Some may say that this young lady simply performed a random act of kindness. I say that she performed an intentional act of leadership.

Choose to reach out to someone with no thought of yourself and you will make a difference!

Watch the Rain

The dark clouds came up rather quickly. People were scurrying to get out of the pouring rain or to run into the rain to get to their cars. I found a comfortable chair and I sat. We were attending a conference in a beautiful beach resort setting and my wife and I arrived a couple of days early to spend some time together and get some rest.

> "We must find the time to stop and allow our bodies, minds, and souls to renew."

As people hurried back and forth, I realized a wonderful feeling... I did not have to be anywhere at anytime that entire day! So I relaxed, sat back and watched the rain. It poured from the sky and as it fell, my soul and mind began to renew.

I did not check my phone, email, text, Twitter, Skype, Instagram, Facebook, Pinterest ...you get the idea. It was refreshing, calming and energizing.

How long has it been since you had nowhere to be? If our leadership is going to remain fresh, innovative and creative, we must find the time to stop and allow our bodies, minds and souls to

renew. It doesn't have to be long sabbaticals (though that would be nice), but times of short duration with the intention of slowing down and unplugging our lives.

The major problem we as leaders have with this concept is guilt. We struggle to give ourselves permission to stop and relax.

We have convinced ourselves that our people need us and we must be available and engaged every minute of every day or.... And that is the question isn't it? "Or what?" The world will end? Our business will crumble? We will lose our job? What is it that drives us to stay eternally connected to our work? Is it a need to be needed?

I don't know about you, but I struggle with finding the time to stop the clock. I think that may be the problem...finding the time. I can search and wait and look but the time never seems quite right for me to allow myself to slow down and relax.

Instead of trying to find the time, I suggest that we make the time. We talk about being intentional in leading others. Perhaps it is time that we focus on leading ourselves. Don't think this will be easy, it will not. However, it is important and necessary if we are going to be strong and effective leaders.

Make the time to "watch the rain" and you will make a difference.

Don't Stare

Bobby may or may not have finished high school. He worked in a manufacturing plant for years until it closed. Then he began his career in sales. From real estate to cars, Bobby sells them all. He now is pushing seventy and has a lifetime of education and leadership knowledge. We were visiting recently when he said, "An old man once told me that it was ok to look back at the past... just don't stare". He said, "I have tried to live by that rule. I can't help what has happened in the past, but I can learn from it and move on".

Things happen in life that are good and bad. While we can't change our past, we do have the opportunity to learn from the past. There is a balance between living in the past and totally disregarding the past. Learning from our past makes us better leaders.

Many times we find ourselves in this rat race of life running from one thing to another without taking the time to slow down and look over our shoulder at where we have been. This blind racing results in us making the same mistakes over and over, or not leveraging things that will make us stronger and more effective leaders.

Choose to take the time to look at your past and learn valuable lessons. Remember, as Bobby says, "don't stare" and you will make a differenc

"It's ok to look back at the past– just don't stare."

Choice

What type of personality makes the best leader?

Is it the extrovert who has charisma and is well spoken? Is it the hard-nosed driver who can get things done? How about the competent leader who pays attention to all of the details of a project or plan? What about the wise soft-spoken leader who can see all of the angles and possesses much wisdom?

The truth is that any and all of the aforementioned personalities can lead well.

The question should not be which personality makes the best leader. The question is: what is the key ingredient for successful leadership?

The answer is: choice. Every leader has the ability to choose how they lead.

Will they choose to become a lifelong learner? Will they choose to become aware of their personality's weaknesses as well as their strengths? Will they choose to develop the ability to connect with and to learn about those who have a different personality than their own? Will they choose to lead with humility?

Successful leaders come in all shapes and sizes and have diverse personalities.

The question for us is simply—will we choose to make a difference?

Unconditional

Some things hit close to home. I watched as this senior executive and entrepreneur walked a very difficult journey towards death. It was not his death he was walking toward, it was the woman that he loves.

As he walked through the last days of her life, his strength grew and he displayed a commitment that could only come through a strong faith and a passionate heart.

I spoke with this seasoned leader after the passing of his loved one and he said, "I knew that this was my time to serve the one I love. There are times when we do what we don't feel like doing because we are called to do them." He went on to describe how he had grown through this journey and was honored to walk with his loved one to the gates of eternity.

His loss was devastatingly tragic; his loved one was a beautiful woman who lost the battle with the demon of cancer. I know of his journey because she was a close family member. I came away from our recent conversation with a renewed desire to display loyalty and love to those within my circle of influence.

When the road is smooth it is easy to display strong leadership. When the journey becomes treacherous and the path is difficult, it is easier to walk away or abdicate our responsibilities to someone else.

Having the courage to lead when the going gets tough exemplifies someone who is committed to speaking into the lives of others. Thank you Rick, for speaking into many of our lives by your leadership and love for Lyn.

When we choose to lead unconditionally we will make a difference.

The Zip-line

> "Leadership is about being willing to acknowledge the success and help of others with gratitude."

I was on a metal chord, dangling what felt like miles above the earth. As I zipped through the air, I felt the exhilaration of the wind, the speed, and height all coming together at once.

Somehow, I talked my wife into zip-lining over the Chattahoochee River as a way of celebrating our 32nd wedding anniversary. I was loving every second of the adventure and she loved it when we arrived safely on the other side of the river. Arriving safely was, however, a bit of a concern.

I realized in mid-flight that we were gaining speed and quickly traveling toward a large tower, where the only thing keeping us from crashing head-first into the massive structure was two staff members, waiting there to catch us. Amazingly, they slowed us down and guided us to safety with skilled expertise.

Upon touching land again, we both acknowledged their efforts with "thanks for doing a great job!" Both young workers immediately told us that we were the first ones to say thanks all day and that it really made them feel good.

Think about that for a minute, two people who literally have hundreds of customers' lives in their hands and no one slows down long enough to say thank you. This was a stark reminder to me of the overall lack of gratitude that we show as a society.

It is logical that the less we show appreciation, the more our relationships on all levels will struggle. Leadership is about being willing to acknowledge the success and help of others with gratitude.

Taking the time to simply say thank you will go a long way toward impacting the lives of those you love, live with and lead.

Choose to reach out and show gratitude to others and you will make a difference!

The Snake Incident

It was exactly how you do not want to end your day. As I pulled down our drive, I met my wife who was walking our small dog.

She paused by our retaining wall as I was slowly passing by. That's when I saw it.

Something long (about 5 feet), round and black came off of the wall toward my wife. Realizing that a snake was wrapped around her arm she bravely threw it off and then explained to me that I needed to take care of this issue.

One thing was certain; my priorities for the evening suddenly were changed.

In a world of corporate and business leadership dilemmas, this adventure reminded me that we can't predict or control what we will face at any moment.

It also reminded me that my priorities can change in an instant... and so can yours.

Choose to remember that life is full of surprises, good and bad, and you will make a difference.

When We Fail

It was failing. There was no doubt that the huge risk taken by the CEO was not going to pay off. The lost resources financially, in personnel and in production time, were large.

With the project spiraling downward, all eyes were on this CEO. How he chose to handle this difficult situation would go a long way toward defining his legacy as a leader with the company. Here's what he did:

Owned It: This leader did blame others but admitted that his project had failed. He took responsibility and recognized the loss.

Created Clarity: He communicated to the entire team that while the project was not successful; the philosophy of taking calculated risks would continue to be a part of the company's growth strategy.

Showed Class: He did not pout, become negative or critical. Instead he remained positive and focused on the future. This executive refused to allow a set back to cause him to lose focus of the overall vision and mission of the organization.

I observed this process first hand, walking with this leader and his organization during this difficult time.

The result of his strong and wise leadership, along with hard work, was record growth over the next year. This failed project did not derail the company but spurred the team to achieve great things.

Leaders who navigate loss with class and honesty are leaders who will make a difference.

168

A wise and experienced leader reminded me of something that we all have in common. We all have 168 hours in a week. Then he challenged me with this question: "How will you live those hours?" If we take a close look at those who are truly successful as leaders, we see that they live their 168 with purpose and meaning.

This leader proposed that the answer could be found in one word - discipline. He said, "Discipline is doing what you don't want to do when you don't want to do it". Think about that for a moment...doing what we don't want to do. It is the secret to living a life of purpose. Choosing to do what is, at times, difficult, time consuming or inconvenient. Not

following our desire for taking the short cut or thinking only of ourselves is where we start. Choosing how we spend our time gives us leverage to make wise decisions and focus our energy in the right direction.

How are you spending your 168? Are you allowing obstacles and distractions to stop you from accomplishing your passion and dreams? Are you allowing yourself to waste your hours of living? As leaders we all have one thing in common, a limited amount of time to influence others.

Choose to start doing the things that you don't want to do...when you don't want to do them and you will make a difference!

Look Beyond the Seaweed

The beach is a place that speaks to my soul. I love the rhythm of the waves, the beauty of the sand dunes, the majesty of a sun setting and the distinctive slow pace that causes me to take pause. A leader friend of mine shares this love for the coast.

On a recent beach excursion with her husband, she reported that upon arriving, they discovered the beach was littered with seaweed. However, instead of allowing that obstacle to ruin their trip they made a choice.

She said, "We decided to look past the seaweed to the beauty of the ocean."

Leading others sometimes gets messy. We find ourselves presented with difficult decisions and hard choices. The truth is that if we are effective leaders our burden gets heavy from time-to-time.

We often find ourselves looking successful, and at other times, wondering how we could have failed so miserably.

Things don't always go the way we planned. It is at these times that we must look beyond the mess that is hitting us in the face to the vision, value, and mission of why we do what we do.

As leaders we have a responsibility to continue the journey of leading well. This means keeping our eye on the horizon of the big picture.

Look beyond the seaweed in your life and you will make a difference!

Waffle House

An executive I was recently talking with shared a personal but incredibly relevant story. Her mother is elderly and is struggling with the vicious disease of Alzheimer's.

This executive regularly takes her mom on day trips in order for them to spend time together.

This trip was to the local Waffle House, a favorite of her mother's. While they were eating, an older man came up to her mom and said, "what a beautiful smile you have". He gently touched her hand and went on his way.

She was a bit confused but no doubt enjoyed the fact that she had just been given a sweet compliment by a stranger.

They continued their meal as another gentleman approached their booth.

He said, "I have been watching you and your mom and it reminded me of the times I took my Dad to do the very same thing. Those are precious memories to me. Thank you for reminding me of those good times. Please allow me to buy your lunch today."

With that, he put a gift of cash on the table and walked away. The executive was moved and appreciated the kind gestures of the two strangers.

Then she saw them. Across the restaurant there sat a young family. She took the cash and paid the gift forward, providing the family the gift of their meal.

What a great example of how we are to lead. Out of our leadership should flow opportunities to give as well as the humility to receive.

This executive's leadership on a personal level demonstrated that ability.

"Out of our leadership should flow opportunities to give, as well as the humility to receive."

While leading her loved ones, she graciously allowed others to invest.

All the while she was aware of the importance of "paying it forward" to others.

When we as leaders understand how to give and receive we will make a difference!

Trust

What do you need? Really. Do you want more money? More power or status? More control?

In our overly busy, overly competitive society, it is easy to misinterpret our wants for our needs. There is nothing wrong with fulfilling wants, as long as we understand the difference.

You may want more, but what do you need?

Take a minute and assess your desires. Make sure you are paying attention to the things you really need as a leader. You need respect; you need to be able to connect with those who are in your circle of influence.

You need to be authentic and you need to know how to have healthy conflict. The bottom line is that you need what all great leaders need. You need trust.

Trust is essential in any relationship. Do you have the trust of your team? Do you have the trust of your leaders?

Choose to understand the importance of trust and you will make a difference!

"How we handle our failures sends a clear and important message to our team, and those we value. It is a glimpse into our souls and our personal foundation."

Leading Through Failure

It was a stark difference. Two leaders, both extremely bright and talented in their fields, had a completely different response.

Each one had been called into a meeting with their boss. The news was hard and pointed. Their teams had simply dropped the ball and the consequence had a significant impact on the company.

The first leader took the news hard, lowered his head and then offered a myriad of excuses for the underperformance of his team.

The second leader listened intently, and then replied, "I take full responsibility". She then asked for a second meeting with her boss to bring back ideas and plans that might mitigate the loss.

While the first leader was busy complaining that he had been treated unfairly, the second was holding meetings with her team and asking the question, "What else can we do".

Failing is a given if you are in leadership for any length of time. There will be those times when your ideas, plans, thoughts and execution simply fail. It is in those crucial moments that your leadership is refined and your character defined.

How we handle those failures sends a clear and important message to our teams, and those we value. It is a glimpse into our souls and our personal foundation.

When we complain and blame others, we set an example of that unhealthy behavior for others to follow.

When we are accountable to own our mistakes, and then look to find ways to correct or navigate the failure, we set an example of a strong and authentic leader.

> *"She was holding meetings with her team and asking 'What else can we do?'"*

Consider pursuing the question "what else can we do" when you are faced with obstacles that look like defeat. Then put action to your words and demonstrate the tenacity and determination that leads to successful leadership on all levels.

It's easy to discern which of the above leaders will rise to gain more responsibility within her company.

Choose to lead through your failures and you will make a difference!

The Practice

A long time leader and executive said something recently that caught my attention. This seasoned veteran with over 37 years of leadership experience in one of the worlds largest and most respected companies said this, "Leadership is a practice...not a position".

Now we all agree that positional leadership is a flawed and ineffective method of influencing others, but the thought that we should "practice " leadership is a bit novel.

That means that we should approach our leading others much like a good physician approaches his or her life's work. A thorough assessment, taking the time to understand the complex needs of each unique individual and developing a path forward are key ingredients to success. It also means understanding that this is "practice " and we will not be perfect in our efforts.

Effective leaders practice investing in their team. They are life-long learners who practice the process of continuous improvement in the area of leading others.

They practice becoming self-aware of their strengths, weaknesses and responses in diverse situations. They practice taking the time to understand the unique make-up of their team. They practice building strong relationships. They practice communicating their vision, and leading with purpose.

Most importantly, they realize that the ability to practice leadership comes with a responsibility similar to the Hippocratic oath to "do no harm" or in other words "lead with integrity".

Choose to practice effective leadership and you will make a difference!

64

Transitional Leadership

At an annual executive leadership forum that I hold annually, one leader shared the "rest of the story". The year before, he had stood and told the group that he was going to lose his job. He was a VP for a very large corporation and because of circumstances beyond his control he was going to be terminated when his current project was completed. He listened as the group gave sound advice on how to approach this dilemma. He was challenged to "finish the play".

He completed his project with such integrity and competency that the company asked him to stay on in another capacity, which he agreed to do. Another large company observed how this executive navigated change and offered him the opportunity to lead their team as Vice President and General Manager. He is now leading this new team with enthusiasm and wisdom.

This leader faced a crisis in his professional career and made a choice to finish the play. His character and leadership ability was most evident in the spotlight of the crisis. Change is inevitable and at times it will be difficult. How will you write the rest of your story? While you may not be able to control the ending, you can control how you respond and walk through each opportunity of change.

Choose to lead through transitions in your life with strength and integrity and you will make a difference!

Stepping Back

She was a young gun. Loaded with all the right stuff, this leader was poised to lead at the executive level one day.

She was smart, hard working, level headed and humble. In just a few short years she had gained the respect of team members who were twice her age.

Her leadership track was headed toward advancement and she was adding value in each role she was assigned.

She asked to meet with her boss and this is what she said, "I realize that it would not be best for this organization or myself to continue in a leadership role. I have carefully considered every angle of my life and I need to step back into a team role at this time".

She went on to share how and why she came to this decision.

This courageous millennial leader was demonstrating the very core fabric of strong leadership: knowing when to step forward and when to step back.

Instead of selfishly remaining in a leadership role for which she was not ready to hold, this young leader chose to step aside. This is a clear picture of integrity.

It would be a mistake to believe that this young lady is no longer a leader or that she has gone away for good.
There will be another season, as she is becoming an incredible leader who influences many others.

For now, she is leading herself and those with whom she comes in contact on a daily basis.

Every once in a while, we all need to take a step back.

> *"She is leading herself and those with whom she comes in contact on a daily basis.*

Having the discernment to take that step means developing a strong self-awareness as well as an authentic concern for those you are leading.

It was a good reminder to me that before we can lead others, we must lead ourselves.

Choose to have the courage to step back and you will make a difference!

It's Not Enough

> "We lead by investing our time, energy and resources in those who desperately need our help."

It's not enough to say that we are " grateful".

Each year Thanksgiving comes and goes and we do our moral and civic duty by spending time with family, giving thanks for our blessings, and indulging ourselves in the consumption of turkey and dressing and all the fixings. These are not bad things; in fact they are good and enjoyable during this season. But those things are not enough.

As Americans, we are one of the wealthiest nations on earth. Many of us make more money in one week than many of our global neighbors make in a year. If you have clean water, sufficient food and clothes, a roof over your head, access to medicine, a mode of transportation and the ability to read a book, then, relative to billions of people in the world, you are rich.

In my town, we have homeless people living behind a well-known grocery store. We have untold numbers of children who are at risk because their parents have neglected or abandoned them on multiple levels. We have gangs trying to find value by invoking violence and chaos.

This is not a black or white, Hispanic or Asian problem. This is an apathy problem. It's not enough to just be glad we are haves and not the have-nots. It's time that we commit to invest our time, energy and resources by investing in those who desperately need our help. Moreover, the old argument that they don't deserve help just doesn't hold true. Not one of us deserves the blessings that we have been given.

It's time for leaders to demonstrate their generosity. Demonstrate gratitude by giving to someone else.

Choose to do more than simply saying you are grateful and you will make a difference.

Who Are You?

While sharing his story, this leader made a comment that struck a chord with me. He said, "Many people allow their identity to become their position."

How many times have we seen leaders who find their identity in their position? No wonder we are struggling for solid strong leadership within our society today. When a leader is defined by title or position alone, character is challenged and relationships are lost.

I have witnessed the above leader as he walked through good times and bad. I knew him before he was elected to his current position. His values and identity have remained the same. He does not receive his validation from his role and he does not make decisions based on current trends or popularity contests. He is defined by his character not his title.

Think about who you would be without your position or title. I believe an effective leader is one who leads the same regardless of his or her circumstances.

Choose to not be defined by your position and you will make a difference.

Who Can Lead?

It's the age-old question: "Can leadership be taught or is it something you are born with?" Companies across the world design their corporate ladders, performance reviews and pay scales on this question. Unfortunately, many times this leads to shortsighted thinking and worse, low or under-achieving performance.

A leader friend of mine sent me an intriguing article recently. It gave evidence that showed when companies make assumptions on who can lead and who cannot, the results can be devastating. In others words, assuming that only those who rank a high performance measure in the metrics arena should be rewarded can cause us to overlook those who have potential but are underachieving. When we lead with numbers and tactical data only, we miss the intangible opportunities to develop and invest in others.

I'm not a proponent of rewarding those who lack work ethic, responsibility or even capacity. I realize that there are times to prune and make hard calls on who are a good fit for our team. However, many times, we may be quick to look at the performance scale and assume the top 20 percent are our leaders and the bottom 20 percent are the loafers. This leaves the mid 60 percent as average achievers. This assumption thinking causes us to make decisions that may not be in the best interest of our organization.

Enough of the statistical analysis: here is the bottom line. We all have potential to lead and contribute on different levels. The question is not "are strong leaders born?" but "are you willing to invest to become the best leader you can be starting with leading yourself?"

It is really just good old common sense that we learned from our grandparents' generation. Every day brings an opportunity for us to grow personally and invest in others. This is true through hard times as well as seasons of smooth sailing.

> "We all have the potential to lead and contribute on different levels."

Leadership is about our desire to be the very best we can be for others and ourselves. What would it be like if our performance reviews, metrics and pay scales reflected not just numbers and percentages but included the intangible measurement of growth and investing?

It's just a thought... but I believe when we strive to achieve our potential in combination with the commitment to help others achieve theirs, we will make a difference!

Behind Bars

She wants to continue her education. She feels a responsibility to those around her. Ann is taking a class on global issues and becoming more aware of the plight of others. What is unique about Ann is that she is 67 years old. She has lived a hard life and has no family, friends or acquaintances that she sees...ever.

Ann is an inmate at a Federal Prison. She has spent the last 30 plus years behind bars and will spend the rest of her life that way. She committed a crime that very likely would have resulted in a different sentence in today's court. But there she is, serving her time and choosing to have the courage to continue to learn and grow even in a correctional institution.

A young leader met Ann as she was teaching at a women's penitentiary on a weekly basis. She told me she wanted to make a difference in the lives of those who have been forgotten. So this leader chose to drive over an hour one-way to teach a group of inmates, one of which was Ann. No one will ever know the impact, great or small that this young 20-something leader made on those women. For some it was just a way to kill time, but perhaps for others it was a small gesture of hope, connection, and humanity.

Leadership is about more than building wealth, power or a moment of fame. It is defined by one's life and commitment to speak into the lives of others.

Ann asked this young woman who was teaching to keep a copy of her graduate certificate that was supposed to be given to her family. She knew no one cared about her achievement, no one, except this young business leader who chose to invest in others.

Choose to take the time to care and you will make a difference.

The Gift of Grits

You've heard it said, "The most effective leaders are those who are driven". I have walked with these driven leaders who have diverse personalities and backgrounds. Some are incredibly wealthy while others are not. Some are CEOs of billion dollar enterprises and others are entrepreneurs leading small start-up businesses. Each of these leaders has experienced highs and lows in their lives. All have won and lost as they traveled their leadership journey.

The question that comes to mind is not *if* they driven but *what is it* that drives these leaders? Recently, I was talking to a wonderful senior adult who has been married for 55 years. She was preparing a breakfast of homemade grits for her husband. I have watched this lady lead others for many years. Her community, friends and especially her family love her. Through the years she has created a legacy of caring for others. As she was working on this southern delicacy, I asked why she chose to get up early and cook grits. Her answer spoke volumes to me. She said, "I found that happiness and joy can truly be found when you can make those you love and care about happy."

When we are driven from a self-gratifying perspective, we lose the right to speak into the lives of others. When our leadership is about our success and our recognition, we send a strong signal to others that we are not worthy of being followed. The leaders who define success by undergirding, protecting, removing obstacles and yes, serving their teams are those who are building a legacy of powerful, effective influence.

This sweet young senior adult has a legacy of love and leadership that will outlive her years on this earth. Thanks Sylvia, for your inspiration and love.

Choose to put the well being of those you lead above your own ambitions and you will make a difference!

"Happiness and joy can truly be found
when you can make those you love
and care about happy."

The Greatest Leader

"His purpose was, and is, to offer a way to God through an authentic relationship with Him."

During the holiday season, we all choose how we celebrate and in which holidays we will participate. I choose to celebrate Christmas. As a follower of Jesus, I pause to reflect on his birth, as that is where my faith begins. With respect for those of other faiths or those who recognize no faith, I embrace your choice to celebrate and worship in the way that is most authentic for you. I would like to share with you why I choose to follow the greatest leader who was ever born.

Jesus is not a religion or particular church. He is not a denomination, organization, or sect. He is not a theological symbol or a complicated spiritual process. Jesus was born for one purpose, and that is to develop relationship with us. His purpose was, and is, to offer a way to God through an authentic relationship with Him.

Jesus asks me, and all of us, to do 3 things: Love God, Love Others and Follow Him. Followers of Jesus come in all shapes and sizes. They are from diverse socio-economical, geographical and cultural backgrounds. They make up a variety of political and social mindsets.

While religious style, preference and even conviction can be debated; one thing cannot be contested. A mountain of evidence and factual accounts supports it. Jesus, who was born in a small cave outside of a crowded inn, grew up to be the greatest leader who ever lived. His movement is unparalleled and his followers continue to expand around the world.

So during the holiday season I will celebrate His birth and how I experience His grace, wisdom, and love in my life. As a follower of Jesus, I will continue to learn about His leadership and more importantly about how He invested in the lives of others.

It is my hope and prayer that the Greatest Leader who ever lived will make a difference in your life.

74

Curve Ahead

The sign said "35 mph" with a curve ahead.

"Don't slow down, in fact speed up " he said. It was the first time I had driven this car but the sales representative was confident in his product. I did what he said and the car took the curve beautifully. It was a defining moment for me and now that automobile sits in my garage.

While I'm not advocating speeding (although my wife would say that I drive too fast at times), I had to make a decision to drive into the curve to experience the performance of that automobile.

As we turn the corner into a new year we must answer an important question in our leadership and lives. What is it that defines you? Are you defined by your education, experience or skill? Are you defined by your success? Do your failures hang around your neck, weighing you

down and keeping you from accelerating into the future? The truth is that none of these things should define us.

I will be defined as someone who loves life and loves people. I refuse to find my internal value from things that are measured by our fickle and inconsistent society. I will not allow my successes or failures to serve as a predictor of my identity. I will instead use both as opportunities for growth. While I realize the importance of caution and care, I will hit the curves of a new year with vigor and confidence in who I am. And, perhaps most importantly, I will refuse to live in the past.

A new year brings new opportunities, new successes and certainly some failures. However, as I accelerate toward this New Year I will not allow any events, good or bad, to define me.

I will lead with confidence in my identity while pursuing my passion... to make a difference in the lives of others.

Dr. Larry Little

Larry Little is the CEO of Eagle Center for Leadership and author of the Make A Difference leadership series. Through his work as a public speaker, facilitator and executive coach, he has served leaders from every walk of life. He and the Eagle Consulting team provide leadership training world wide. Larry's purpose is to make a difference in the lives of others both professionally and personally. His hope for you is that you will come to understand leadership at its truest form.

Larry lives in his hometown of Decatur, Alabama with his wife, Melanie. They have two grown children, Lauren and Landon, who he enjoys vacationing with at his favorite place in the world, the beach at Gulf Shores. He loves chocolate pie, reading lots of books, and listening to the music of the Eagles. Some of his best leadership lessons come from watching The Andy Griffith Show, and he is a die-hard Auburn Tigers fan.

Larry's next leadership adventure is to take his leadership philosophy and the Make A Difference framework to the next level by continuing to develop a connection with leaders around the world, using virtual tools as well as personal investment.

You can learn more about Larry, Make A Difference, and Eagle Center for Leadership by visiting:

www.eaglecenterforleadership.com

You can also use the link above to take the Make A Difference personality profile, and take a step forward in your own leadership journey.

CPSIA information can be obtained
at www.ICGtesting.com
Printed in the USA
LVHW07n2122221018
594430LV00001B/2/P